A Young Nation Develops

by Moehle and Mitchell

Illustrated by Helen Hausner and Larry Weaver

In this series we have attempted to present a general view of the growth of the United States as a democratic republic. We have tried to present the major events of historical importance, as well as the figures who were involved in them. Through the use of visual material, the printed page, and student activities, it is hoped that the students will enjoy the presentation of history as a meaningful and ever continuing experience.

CONTENTS

Indicates full-color transparencies

MILLIKEN PUBLISHING CO.

TO THE TEACHER:

This book ios a new approach to the presentation of American history as a vital ongoing experience. By means of twelve colorful transparencies and reproducible pages, the panoramic aspects of our nation's history have been presented, using text, maps, and visuals. The material has been designed to stimulate discussion and create a desire for more detailed study. Activities and test pages have been included to help the student check his grasp of the concepts and to aid the teacher in measuiring the progress of the class.

SUGGESTED ACTIVITIES:

For those teachers using a unit or core approach, the following activities are suggested to be used in correlating the material with other subject matter areas.

1. "Histo-provisations" — These improvised conversations can be between two famous figures or between average citizens of the period. Students should be urged to review the major topics and issues of the time and to use this information in their dialogue. If the student is representing a specific person, he can use famous quotations or paraphrases if they are applicable to the situation presented.

   The following situations may prove helpful:
   a. Thomas Jefferson instructs Livingston on his mission to France
   b. An American is denied the right of deposit by a French official at New Orleans
   c. Two New Englanders discuss the War Hawks
   d. James Monroe announces his doctrine
   e. A plantation owner instructs his overseer
   f. A factory worker talks about his new way of life
   g. A northern manufacturer and a southern planter discuss tariffs
2. Have students prepare "eye witness" news broadcasts of historical events.
   a. The burning of Washington
   b. The shelling of Fort McHenry
   c. The announcement of the Monroe Doctrine
   d. An abolitionist meeting featuring a speech by Frederick Douglas or Sojourner Truth
3. Have students prepare a newspaper dealing with the War of 1812. They should include news articles, editorials, letters to the editor and editorial cartoons.
4. Have students do soap or sawdust chip carvings to simulate the carvings done by the early whalers.

5. Have students make paper or balsa models of whaling ships or clipper ships. If this is not practical, watercolor wash paintings of ships might be done.
6. Have students prepare a display in miniature of costumes worn by the various classes of southern society: plantation owner and family, slaves, town dweller, mountain whites.
7. Have two teams of students research and debate the current pros and cons of protective tariffs.
8. Have student committees prepare reports with appropriate graphics on Canada, Our Northern Neighbor.
   a. Geography
   b. Industry
   c. Cultural life
   d. French Canada
   e. Present United States—Canadian relations
   f. Government
9. Have students prepare a comedy melodrama of life in the mountains, i.e. feuds, distrust of city folk, etc.
10. Have students make dioramas or shoebox models of early factories.
11. Have students research and report on the growth of labor unions in the United States.
12. Have students make models of a plantation and a medieval manor showing similarities and differences between them.
13. Have students research the presidential elections of the period and make campaign posters supporting the various candidates.
14. Build a unit on Negro spirituals. Include any of the so-called white spirituals that appeal to students. See Jolin Jacob Niles Collection for suggestions.
15. Introduce poems of the period or related to the period.

Page 1 — THE LOUISIANA PURCHASE
TO THINK ABOUT

1. France hoped that she would someday be able to rebuild an empire in North America and planned to use the Mississippi as a main waterway.
2. Jefferson believed that England might demand too much in return for their support. He feared that the United States could again become too dependent on England.
3. The Napoleonic Wars pitted France against the major powers of Europe. These wars depleted both the French treasury and its military ranks. Napoleon knew that he needed money. He also knew that he did not have the military strength to prevent the United States from taking New Orleans by force.
4. a. Toussaint L'Ouverture was a slave who became the leader of a revolt on the island of Santo Domingo in the West Indies. Napoleon planned to use Santo Domingo as a naval base in his scheme to rebuild an empire in

the New World. The revolt led by L'Ouverture was one of the bloodiest slave rebellions in history.

    b. When Napoleon could not put down the rebellion, he began to lose his appetite for an empire in the New World and decided to sell Louisiana to the United States.

5. a. Nepotism is the act of showing favoritism to relatives, especially in filling political positions.

5. b. Napoleon's brothers were made heads of state: Joseph Bonaparte was made King of Naples and later King of Spain, Louis Bonaparte was King of Holland, Jerome Bonaparte was King of Westphalia and Lucian Bonaparte was a chief minister of the French government.

*Page 1A — THE UNITED STATES IN 1803

This map should be shown and discussed. The area included in the Louisiana Purchase should be pointed out, as well as the areas still belonging to Spain, Britain, etc.

Page 2 — TROUBLE WITH BRITAIN
TO THINK ABOUT

1. Britain impressed Americans and seized American ships, and France confiscated cargoes.
2. a. Those Americans who believed in the theory of manifest destiny told themselves that it was the destiny of the American people to inhabit and govern a continental empire stretching from coast to coast.
   b. Answers will vary.
3. a. Hawks are warlike birds who prey on small birds.
   b. A dove is the symbol of peace
4. The Embargo Act succeeded only in preventing American merchants from selling merchandise and keeping many men unemployed.
5. Answers will vary greatly. Several of the speeches might be given to the class. The effectiveness and validity of each speech might be discussed.

Page 3 — AN UNPOPULAR WAR

The influence of the War Hawks, the opposition to the war, the Hartford Convention and its results, the attitude of the American people, and the fact that the United States was not prepared to fight a war should be emphasized. The profound effect produced by the attitude of the War Hawks and the war on the relations between Canada and the United States should also be stressed.

Page 4 — ACTIVITY SHEET

I — HISTORY WORDS TO KNOW

ceded — relinquished by treaty

frigate — a fast sailing vessel which carried from twenty to forty guns

negotiations — mutual discussions for the arrangement of the terms of a transaction or agreement

alleged — supposed; declared to be

depleted — decreased seriously; exhausted the supply

proclamation — an official announcement or declaration

nepotism — favoritism shown on the basis of family relationship, especially in politics

neutrality — the status of a nation which does not take part or give assistance in a war between other nations

impress — to force into public service, usually as seamen

right of deposit — written permission to store specified items until a certain time

grievances — complaints; circumstances regarded as just causes for protest

confederation — an alliance of states or nations

embargo — a government order prohibiting the movement of merchant ships into or out of its ports

doctrine — a particular principle, position, or policy that is advocated

inciting — urging on; stimulating

repealed — revoked or withdrawn formally or officially

manifest destiny — a belief that the United States should extend from the Atlantic to the Pacific

advocate — to plead in favor of; support

blockade — the use of ships or troops by one nation to close off the ports or borders of another nation

secession — the withdrawing of a state from a national union

contraband — anything prohibited by law from being imported or exported

annex — to incorporate into an existing country or state

II — TO THINK ABOUT

1. a. Lack of funds, poor military leaders, no citizen support.
   b. Answers will vary.
2. The war threatened their economy which was based on trade with England.
3. Its purpose was to declare opposition to the War of 1812.
4. a. The withdrawing of a state from a national union.
   b. A state could threaten to leave the Union any and every time it was displeased with a law, etc.
   c. The Civil War
5. Most Canadians felt that if impressment was the issue, the quarrel was with England and not with Canada. Canadians resented the American attempts to seize their lands.

III — RESEARCH TOPICS

Students might prepare oral or written reports on those subjects which interest them most.

Page 5 — THE WAR OF 1812 — I
MATCHING

___ 1. William Hull
_e_ 2. Oliver Perry
_a_ 3. Winfield Scott
_b_ 4. Thomas Macdonough
_c_ 5. Francis Scott Key
_d_ 6. William Henry Harrison

*Page 5A — THE WAR OF 1812

This transparency should be shown and discussed as the various phases of the war are studied. Have students tell why Clay and Calhoun are pictured here.

Page 6 — THE WAR OF 1812 — II
TO THINK ABOUT

1. The Declaration of Independence, the Constitution, Washington's Farewell Address, and others.
2. Answers will vary but should be complete and accurate.
3. The music written to complement Key's poem is difficult to sing because of its extremely wide range. There are also those who think certain parts of Key's poem are too violent and warlike.
4. The British ships greatly outnumbered the American vessels.
5. Answers will vary.
6. Nothing was accomplished or settled by the War of 1812.

Page 7 — A CROSSWORD PUZZLE

A. Complete the word puzzle using the word clues given below.

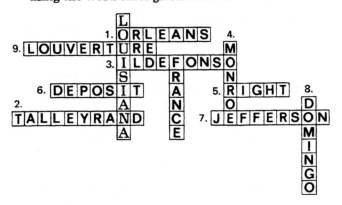

1. New Orleans, an important river port.
2. **Talleyrand**, advisor to Napoleon.
3. The Treaty of **Ildefonso** returned Louisiana to France.
4. James **Monroe**, sent to France to purchase New Orleans.
5. **Right** of 6. **deposit**, permission to unload goods at New Orleans.
7. President **Jefferson** made the Louisiana Purchase.
8. Santo **Domingo**, site of slave uprising.

9. Toussaint **L'Ouverture**, leader of slave uprising.
10. **France**, original owner of Louisiana.

B. Complete these statements to make them true.

11. The **Embargo Act** forbade any American ship to sail for a foreign port.
12. The doctrine of **manifest destiny** said that the United States had to expand to its natural boundaries.
13. **John C. Calhoun** of South Carolina was a leader of the War Hawks.
14. **Commodore Perry** commanded the American Navy on the Great Lakes.
15. The **Hartford Convention** protested the War of 1812.
16. **Dolley Madison** saved many valuable documents from the flames at Washington, D. C.
17. The attack on Fort **McHenry** inspired the Star Spangled Banner.
18. The Battle of New Orleans was won by General **Andrew Jackson**.
19. **Jean Lafitte** was a French pirate who aided the Americans at New Orleans.
20. The **Treaty of Ghent** ended the War of 1812.

Page 8 — THE MONROE DOCTRINE
TO THINK ABOUT

1. a. People who are nationalistic are devoted to the interests of their country. They will fight to defend the rights of that country.
   b. Answers will vary.
2. Unable to obtain articles from England, the United States was forced to manufacture its own.
3. The United States had proved it could protect itself from the strong European powers and the other countries of the Western Hemisphere were weak and helpless.
4. The Monroe Doctrine stated that: no new colonies were to be established in the Western Hemisphere; the United States would not meddle in European affairs; the United States expected the European powers to stop interfering with governments in the Americas.
5. Although the United States stated in the Monroe Doctrine that the Latin American countries were to be free to guide their own destinies, on numerous occasions the United States resorted to "dollar diplomacy" and military occupations to see that these destinies were in the best interests in the United States. This was the case in Panama, Venezuela, Chile, Cuba, and several other Latin American republics.

*Page 8A — THE MONROE DOCTRINE

The provisions of the Monroe Doctrine are illustrated on this transparency. Students should be asked to explain the meaning of the cartoon at the bottom of the page.

Page 9 — TRADE AND MANUFACTURING
REVIEW

1. The economy of New England depended primarily on trade. Many sailors had been killed or had given up the sea. Ships had been lost and the two largest markets — England and the West Indies — were lost to the traders.
2. a. China, Russia, Denmark, Sweden
   b. Those countries on accessible water routes became new trading markets.
3. The Barbary pirates seized merchant ships and cargoes and threatened to put an end to the United States trading in the Mediterranean.
4. The United States again proved that the United States would stand up for its rights and the action against the Barbary pirates gave the United States a new dignity and sense of accomplishment.
5. The original marine uniform had a collar made of leather.

*Page 9A — TRADING

Captain Gray, his importance in establishing new markets, and the Barbary pirates should be discussed as this transparency is shown.

Page 10 — SHIPPING AND WHALING
REVIEW

1. Whaling provided several products which were in great demand and provided work for great numbers of workers.
2. United States ships were unable to safely sail the seas.
3. a & b. Answers will vary.
4. His clipper ship enabled the United States to dominate shipping. These ships were able to cover long distances with great speed.
5. Americans refused to accept the ocean-going steamship which eventually made the clipper ship obsolete.
6. a. Because they did not have to carry a large supply of fuel, the clipper ship was able to carry larger quantities of cargoes. They were, however, dependent on the wind and despite the design of the ship and the tremendous sails there were times when a lack of strong wind was a hindrance.
   b. Because they were not dependent on wind and carried supplies of fuel for the steam engines, they were always assured of an adequate source of power.
7. "Round the horn" was an expression used to describe a trip around Cape Horn.

*Page 10A — SHIPPING AND WHALING

After this transparency is discussed, interested students might wish to read about the hard life of the whalers. Reports might be prepared and given to the class about the rigors of whaling. Students might also wish to prepare graphs and a history of the American Merchant Marine from its beginning to the present. Some students might wish to prepare a display of ship models showing the development of merchant ships.

Page 11 — THE INDUSTRIAL REVOLUTION
I — TO THINK ABOUT

1. a. Mercantilism — the practice of obliging a colony to buy the finished products of the mother country for which the colony originally supplied the raw materials.
   b. If the British had a textile monopoly, the colonies would be forced to sell England the cotton and to buy the manufactured textiles made from that cotton.
2. The time when newly invented machines began replacing hand labor was the period of the Industrial Revolution.
3. a. James Hargreaves invented the spinning jenny.
   b. Richard Arkwright perfected the jenny; his machine could spin eighty spindles at once.
   c. Edmund Cartwright invented a power loom.
   d. James Watt invented the steam engine.
   e. Samuel Crompton invented the spinning mule, a machine that spun cotton into yarn and wound it on spindles.

II — RESEARCH QUESTIONS

1. a. sincerely comes from the Latin sine cerex which means without wax. It was a mark which was put on a statue or sculpture only if the artist had used no wax to patch or conceal a blemish.
   hallmark was a sign or symbol of the goldsmiths' guild, the hall referring to the guild hall to which the goldsmiths belonged.
   b. Sincerely today means free from deceit or falseness; genuinely. Hallmark is a mark of genuineness, and high quality.
2. a. The medieval guilds and unions were both organized according to the type of work done by the workers. Both were interested in improving working conditions and regulating wages, prices, etc. Both were interested in training and perpetuating the skills of their particular craft.
   b. Guilds extended much more completely into the life of guild members and their families. The guild hall was the center of life for members and their families. Social, educational, and even religious activities revolved around the guild. A guild was more or less directly responsible for the welfare of a member during his entire life. Unions, on the other hand, play a vital part of a worker's life only in his occupation. Social activities,

etc., are much less important today. Although most unions do have excellent welfare programs for their members, these are not as all-inclusive as were those of the guilds.

3. Crompton's mule was a spinning machine that spun cotton into yarn and wound it on spindles.

*Page 11A — THE INDUSTRIAL REVOLUTION IN ENGLAND

Interested students might be asked to explain the operation of each of the machines shown on this transparency. The importance of each should also be noted.

Page 12 — REVIEW

I   1. William Henry Harrison
2. James Monroe
3. Stephen Decatur
4. Andrew Jackson
5. Robert Gray
6. Donald McKay
7. James Hargreaves
8. Richard Cartwright
9. Richard Arkwright
10. James Watt

II   11. Monroe Doctrine
12. the *Empress of China* or the *Columbia*
13. Barbary Coast
14. Ambergris
15. the *Flying Cloud*
16. Industrial Revolution
17. spinning jenny
18. the *Columbia*
19. monopoly
20. 1823

Page 13 — MANUFACTURING IN AMERICA — I

TO THINK ABOUT

1. It was important for England's mercantilism that the colonies bought more than they sold. This could best be accomplished by keeping the colonies agricultural rather than industrial.
2. a. <u>artist</u> — one who creates works of art, especially a painter or sculptor
   <u>artisan</u> — one skilled in making a particular commodity; a craftsman
   <u>laborer</u> — one engaged in work which requires bodily strength rather than skill or training
   b. artist
   c. laborer/artisan. Accept either answer which student can justify.
3. a. Self-sufficient — able to supply one's own needs with external assistance
   b. Medieval manors and plantations were both self-sufficient. They both grew their own

food, and had their own carpenters, blacksmiths, etc.
4. These items were needed for the war effort and the raw materials for these articles were readily available.
5. Although the United States had gained political independence, it was unable to become the successful manufacturer and remained the buyer, maintaining England's practice of mercantilism.
6. The Northeast was the only section of the country to gain economically, since the South was forced to sell its cotton to the Northeast instead of to England.

*Page 13A — MANUFACTURING IN AMERICA

The effects of the Industrial Revolution as indicated in the sketches should be discussed. Interested students may wish to report on Samuel Slater and his mill. Students might discuss the invention of machines from the point of view of workers of the period.

Page 14 — MANUFACTURING IN AMERICA — II

TO THINK ABOUT

1. a. Samuel Slater built copies of English machines and built a cotton mill in Pawtucket, Rhode Island. Slater actually brought the Industrial Revolution to America.
   b. Elias Howe invented the sewing machine.
   c. Francis Lowell opened the first complete factory for the manufacture of raw cotton into cotton cloth in Massachusetts.
   d. Robert and Alexander Barr developed machines that could cord, rope, and spin cotton and wool.
2. There were few rushing streams to furnish power in the South and West, less people to work in factories, and people were too busy clearing land and fighting Indians to establish and operate factories.
3. Answers will vary but students will probably state that since England was trying to keep America bound to it economically and attempting to hinder its economic growth, it was not unethical for Americans to use machines patterned after the English models. Accept any reasonable answers.
4. a. A patent is an official document which assures an inventor that he alone has the right to make, use, and sell his invention for a given period of time.
   b. It protects an inventor from the theft of his idea or invention and prevents others from profitting from his work.
   c. A copyright is the exclusive right granted by law to publish, sell, or distribute a literary or musical work. A copyright protects an

author or composer as a patent protects an inventor.

5. a. Mass production makes possible the manufacture of many more items, thereby increasing the availability of such items and reducing their cost.

   b. Workers involved in mass production have less pride in their workmanship and articles are often of poorer quality than hand-crafted items.

HISTORY WORDS TO KNOW

tanner — one who converts hides into leather

textile — cloth; fabric

economy — a system for the management and development of resources

ordnance — military supplies, especially weapons, ammunition; heavy guns; artillery

immigrant — one who settles permanently in a foreign country

mass production — the manufacture of goods in large quantities, using assembly-line techniques

*Page 14A — THE TARIFF

The tax half of this transparency should be explained before students begin to study page 15. They should understand the meaning and the purpose of a tariff. The bottom half of the transparency should be shown and discussed after students have done the work on page 15. Students should be able to tell the Southern, Northern, and English reactions to the tariff.

Page 15 — GOVERNMENT HELP

TO THINK ABOUT

1. Because their methods were perfected and their workers well-trained, numerous, well-made articles were turned out. They were cheaper because the initial cost of the factories and machinery had been absorbed and articles could be sold for less.

2. A protective tariff is a tax placed on manufactured goods brought into a country from a foreign country. Its purpose is to "protect" a country's industries from foreign competition.

3. The West and the South felt that they were being forced to pay higher prices for manufactured articles.

4. a. Article I, Section IX, Paragraph 6 of the United States Constitution states that Congress may not make a law which favors one state or one section of the country.

   b. No, because a tariff is for the good of the country.

   Answers will vary somewhat.

5. If a tariff equalizes the cost of imported and domestic merchandise, domestic manufacturers and their employees benefit, making it possible

for those people to do business with local merchants, etc., etc., etc.

6. The rising tariff laws were "golden" for the Northeast, but were a heavy burden to the South and West. As the tariff became higher and higher, storm clouds began to form in the West and South.

Page 16 — AMERICA CHANGES

REVIEW

1. People moved to communities to work in the factories, merchants, lawyers, doctors, and others moved into the community to provide for and sell to the factory workers and cities began to grow and grow.

2. Bankers, doctors, dentists, lawyers, policemen, etc.

3. Factories were poorly lighted and poorly ventilated; they were hot in the summer and bitter cold in the winter; there were no restrooms and no medical service was available in case of injury.

4. a. Labor unions were formed to improve working conditions in the factories.

   b. Both were interested in improving conditions for the workers.

5. a. Acting on the basis of prejudice, the treatment of a person based on the group, class, or category to which that person belongs rather than on individual merit.

   b. Early factory owners discriminated against women and children.

HISTORY WORDS TO KNOW

consumer — a buyer

competition — a rivalry for profit, prize, or position

tariff — a tax imposed on imported goods

preferential — showing or giving preference

urban — pertaining to a city or town

rural — pertaining to the country

ventilation — the act of providing a room, etc., with fresh air

conveniences — things that save or simplify work or add to a person's ease or comfort

discrimination — acting on the basis of prejudice; the treatment of a person based on the group, class, or category to which that person belongs rather than on individual merit.

Page 17 — TEST AND REVIEW

A.

1. False	8. False
2. True	9. False
3. False	10. True
4. False	11. False
5. True	12. True
6. True	13. True
7. False	14. False

B. 15. a   19. a
    16. c   20. b
    17. c   21. a
    18. c   22. c

23. Opinion question; answers will vary.
24. Getting a patent was time-consuming in those days and many of the machines were simple and easily copied.

Page 18 — CHANGES IN THE SOUTH

REVIEW

1. Because the Industrial Revolution greatly increased production in the textile industry, there was a very great demand for cotton.
2. Because Whitney's cotton gin made the growing of cotton very profitable, he is credited with creating the Cotton Kingdom.
3. A. Mass production
   B. While the cotton gin affected only the cotton growers and industries dependent on cotton, mass production was applied to many industries.
4. Cotton uses many minerals found in the soil and these minerals must be replaced.
5. A. Accept "Cotton is King" or any other appropriate title.
   B. Students should indicate that Southerners (especially plantation owners and aristocrats) worshipped cotton and the wealth it brought. The burden or heavy load was carried by the slaves who made it possible for cotton to be "King."

Page 19 — THE SOUTH EXPANDS

REVIEW

1. New Orleans and Mobile developed into major cities because they were important shipping centers. They were both located on rivers which were the "highways" of the South. Cotton was shipped by river to New Orleans or Mobile and there loaded on ocean-going vessels. Both cities also had excellent harbors which could accommodate large merchant ships.
2. If a group depends on one product for a living and the demand for that product decreases, the group's means of making a liviing is removed.
3. The great demand for cotton and the invention of the cotton gin made slavery imperative.
4. Defenders of slavery argued that slaves were not prepared to support and care for themselves due to their complete lack of education and training. These very "defenders" were responsible for keeping the slaves ignorant and illiterate.
5. Since cotton was the money crop of the South and many Southerners were indirectly affected by the sale of cotton, many felt that they had to defend it. There was also a great deal of sectional loyalty in those days.

6. Answers will vary greatly but an evil act cannot be excused simply by saying that people have been doing it throughout history. History has shown us that civilizations who practiced slavery eventually crumbled because citizens became morally corrupt when they lost their incentive to work.

*Page 19A — THE SOUTH EXPANDS

Students should understand why the South "moved" and where. The meaning of the graph should be discussed. Students might make their own graphs using the information on the one shown here.

Page 20 — THE PLANTATION

REVIEW

1. They controlled all of the wealth in the South, therefore they were very powerful.
2. a. If they were educated and were able to read and write, they would not be content with their lot in life and would be anxious to leave the plantations. Many were well cared for and knew no other life and were content.
   b. Adolph Hitler and his Nazi party burned books so that the people could read only what the Nazis wanted them to read and believe only what they were told to believe. Many iron curtain countries today prohibit the reading of materials from other countries.
3. a. The encomienda system was instituted in Spanish America in 1503. Under this system a Spanish soldier or colonist was granted a tract of land or a village together with its Indian inhabitants.
   b. It resembled the plantation system in that the Indian workers worked for the landowner rather than for themselves. In return the landowner provided certain services and "room and board," so to speak.
4. a. A serf on a manor was not free and worked for the lord of the manor as a slave worked for the plantation owner.
   b. A slave was owned by his master, but a serf belonged to the land; a serf was bound to the soil and when a new lord took over the manor, the serf stayed on.
5. a. The Negro spiritual.
   b. It was a form of expression; they expressed their emotions through music. Their religion taught that only in the afterlife would they be truly free and they sang of the joys of the afterlife. They also preserved the musical culture of their ancestors with their songs.

Page 21 — THE OTHER SOUTH

REVIEW

1. There were few streams to furnish water power

for factories and the South was largely agricultural and rural.

2. Because many of the Southerners were English aristocrats and their descendants, their heritage was steeped in English tradition. They traded a great deal with England and therefore had access to English goods and fashions.
3. They were geographically a part of the South but not culturally or economically. They kept very much to themselves and had little or no contact with or interest in the rest of the South.
4. The geography of the areas in which they settled resembled their homeland.
5. They were economically dependent on the slave system and the cotton growers and they were sectionally Southerners and loyal to their section of the country.

HISTORY WORDS TO KNOW

indigo — a blue dye obtained from various plants
boll — a rounded seed pod of the cotton plant
textile — a woven material
patent — a government grant to an inventor giving him exclusive right to make, use, and sell his invention.
firearm — a small arms weapon from which a projectile is fired by gunpowder
interchangeable — two things capable of being put or used in the place of each other
the Old South — Virginia, Maryland, North Carolina, South Carolina, and Georgia
deplete — decrease seriously or exhaust the supply of or the abundance of something
the Lower South — Alabama, Mississippi, Louisiana.
dominant — governing; ruling; controlling
plantation system — a system is one in which one crop is grown on large tracts of land with slave labor
overseer — foreman in charge of the work on a plantation and the operation of the plantation
dialect — a regional variety of a spoken language
barter — to exchange goods or services without using money
isolation — the complete separation from others

Page 22 — TEST AND REVIEW

A — MATCHING

1.	Q	9.	L
2.	S	10.	B
3.	I	11.	M
4.	A	12.	D
5.	N	13.	O
6.	C	14.	E
7.	J	15.	R
8.	K	16.	H

B — WHO AM I?

17.	an overseer	19.	a mountain white
18.	the master's wife	20.	a slave

Page 23 — SECTIONALISM — I

REVIEW

1. The North depended on manufacturing, trade, and business, while the South relied on cotton to maintain its economy.
2. The factories of the Northeast suffered from seasonal slumps and the factory owners had to provide for the slaves during these slumps as well as during busy seasons. It was not economically sound for them to do so.
3. George Washington, Patrick Henry, and Thomas Jefferson.
4. a. John C. Calhoun
   b. He was a War Hawk who advocated war with England in 1812.
5. a. Because they were willing to work for very low wages.
   b. Immigrants, because they were also willing to work for low wages. There was such an abundance of workers that many who were employed were afraid of losing their jobs.
6. Like the plantation owners and their slaves, the affluent and well-educated still live well while the disadvantaged live poorly and in most cases are still dependent on others for their survival.

*Page 23A — SECTIONALISM

Students should understand the problems, needs, and interests of the three sections of the country. They might wish to make their own sectionalism maps.

Page 24 — SECTIONALISM — II

REVIEW

1. a. Good roads to the frontier and cheap land.
   b. They wanted good roads on which to travel to the West and they wanted the land to be offered at prices they could afford.
2. As the frontier territories became states and entered the Union, the question of whether they would be slave or free states would arise.
3. a. Most Westerners opposed slavery.
   b. Westerners had a strong sense of democracy and equality since on the frontier all men were equal and began their lives on an equal footing.
4. Charts will vary.
5. Students should color the states in the North red, those of the South green, and the Western lands yellow. Students might be asked to write the names of the states (abbreviations may be used) and the dates of their admission to the Union.

Page 25 — THE ABOLITIONISTS

TO THINK ABOUT

1. It is part of the inscription on the Liberty Bell.

2. a. They are slave traders, or Northerners involved in trading slaves
   b. the South
   c. revile — be contemptuous of; speak of abusively
   d. that the northern position on slavery was hypocritical
3. a. A slave revolt occurred in 1831 in Virginia and was led by a slave, Nat Turner. Turner organized a murderous attack on homes in Virginia and about one hundred sixty men of both races were killed in the bloody attack.
   b. The South accused the abolitionists of approving of and encouraging insurrection, murder, and other hideous crimes.

Page 26 — A FINAL TEST AND REVIEW — I

1. a. Napoleon
   b. Talleyrand
   c. ~~L'Ouverture~~

Napoleon and Talleyrand were French; L'Ouverture was a Haitian slave who led a revolt against France.

2. a. ~~Tecumseh~~
   b. Creek
   c. Cherokee

Tecumseh was an Indian chief; Creek and Cherokee are Indian tribes.

3. a. ~~James Madison~~
   b. Henry Clay
   c. Felix Grundy

Madison was not a War Hawk; Clay and Grundy were War Hawks.

4. a. Henry Dearborn
   b. ~~William Eustis~~
   c. William Hull

Eustis was Secretary of War; Dearborn and Hull were generals during the War of 1812.

5. a. William Henry Harrison
   b. Winfield Scott
   c. ~~Oliver Perry~~

Perry was a navy hero; Scott and Harrison were Army heroes.

6. a. Detroit
   b. ~~York~~
   c. Baltimore

York (Toronto) is a Canadian town; Detroit and Baltimore were in the United States.

7. a. *Constitution*
   b. *Old Ironsides*
   c. ~~*United States*~~

Constitution and *Old Ironsides* are names for the same ship.

8. a. Sweden
   b. ~~Tripoli~~
   c. China

Tripoli was not one of the ports with which we opened trade.

9. a. ~~*Flying Cloud*~~
   b. *Empress of China*
   c. *Columbia*

Columbia and *Empress of China* traded with China; *Flying Cloud* was a clipper ship.

10. a. James Hargreaves
    b. ~~Elias Howe~~
    c. Richard Arkwright

Elias Howe was an American inventor; Hargreaves and Arkwright were English inventors.

11. a. Oliver Evans
    b. John Fitch
    c. ~~Francis Lowell~~

Lowell was primarily a factory builder; Evans and Fitch were inventors.

12. a. ~~1812~~
    b. 1824
    c. 1828

1824 and 1828 were tariff years; there was no tariff passed in 1812.

13. a. cotton gin
    b. ~~sewing machine~~
    c. mass production

Cotton gin and mass production were invented by Eli Whitney; he did not invent the sewing machine.

14. a. New Orleans
    b. Mobile
    c. ~~Charleston~~

New Orleans and Mobile were ports of the Lower South; Charleston was not.

15. a. ~~John C. Calhoun~~
    b. Patrick Henry
    c. Thomas Jefferson

Henry and Jefferson denounced slavery; Calhoun advocated slavery.

16. a. Benjamin Lundy
    b. ~~Nat Turner~~
    c. William Lloyd Garrison

Lundy and Garrison were abolitionists; Turner was a slave.

17. a. Frederick Douglass
    b. Sojourner Truth
    c. ~~Angelina Grimke~~

Angelina Grimke was a white abolitionist; Douglass and Truth were former slaves who worked for the abolitionist cause.

Page 27 — A FINAL TEST AND REVIEW — I

1. Robert Livingston
2. West Florida
3. Embargo Act
4. impressment
5. Hartford Convention

6. Tecumseh
7. Jean Lafitte
8. Ghent
9. Monroe Doctrine
10. Robert Gray
11. Stephen Decatur
12. Ambergris
13. Industrial Revolution
14. Elias Howe
15. tariff
16. Liberia
18. abolitionists
19. Lower South
20. mass production
21. William Lloyd Garrison
22. Sojourner Truth
23. John C. Calhoun
24. Francis Scott Key

*Page 27A—BIOGRAPHICAL REVIEW

This transparency may be used as a final quiz or review or as a springboard for oral or written biographies of these people.

The historical figures pictured are (from left to right): Row 1. Stephen Decatur, James Monroe, Oliver Hazard Perry; Row 2. Frederick Douglass, Andrew Jackson, Francis Scott Key; Row 3. Robert Gray, Sojourner Truth, Samuel Slater.

Page 28 — HISTORY WORDS TO KNOW

Students may need several copies of this page to record the words and expressions and their definitions assigned on the pages of this unit. Teachers may wish to add others, depending on the ability of the class.

*Page 28A — HISTORY WORDS TO KNOW

Words and their definitions may be written on the transparency and removed and the transparency used again to teach, review, check pupils' responses, or test.

THE LOUISIANA PURCHASE

As the frontier settlements west of the Appalachian Mountains began to prosper, the trappers and farmers were faced with a problem. In order to make a living they had to get their products to market. The overland routes through the mountains were long and difficult. It was much easier to float the goods down the Ohio River to the Mississippi River and then down to the port of New Orleans. The frontiersmen used rafts and flatboats to reach New Orleans. There they were given the <u>right of deposit</u>. This meant that their goods could be loaded on ships which would sail for the east coast of the United States or directly to European ports.

The Mississippi River did not belong to the United States. It marked the boundary between the United States and the Spanish territory to the west. This territory had been ceded to Spain by France near the end of the French and Indian War to keep it from falling into English hands. There was a mutual understanding that one day France would reclaim the Louisiana Territory.

As long as Spain controlled New Orleans, Americans were allowed the right of deposit freely or for a small fee. They did not know what would happen when France reclaimed the area.

In 1800, Spain and France signed the Treaty of Ildefonso. This document transferred the Louisiana Territory and New Orleans back to France. Americans then found the port of New Orleans closed to them, and they appealed to the United States government for help.

President Jefferson understood the economic hardship the farmers faced, and he also recognized the dangerous possibility that Napoleon might be planning to expand the French territory in North America. If this happened, Jefferson knew that he would be driven into an alliance with England. He wanted to avoid such an alliance at all costs.

In 1803, Jefferson sent James Monroe to Paris to join Robert Livingston in negotiations concerning New Orleans. Monroe was authorized to offer $10,000,000 for New Orleans and the piece of land called West Florida. If the offer was refused, Monroe was to suggest that the United States would take the land by force, if necessary.

Napoleon was having difficulties of his own. His European wars had depleted the treasury. On the island of Santo Domingo in the West Indies, a slave revolt led by Toussaint L'Ouverture threatened to cut off France's supply of sugar, coffee, and cotton. A large French army under the command of Napoleon's brother-in-law, Charles Leclerc, was unable to stamp out the rebellion.

Talleyrand, one of Napoleon's advisors, wisely advised Napoleon to let the Americans have, not only New Orleans, but all of the Louisiana Territory, as well. The French knew that it would be impossible for them to hold it by force.

Napoleon offered the Americans the entire land mass (not including West Florida) for fifteen million dollars. The surprised Americans quickly accepted Napoleon's offer.

Jefferson, who believed in the strict interpretation of the Constitution, was not certain that he had the power to acquire land in this manner. Jefferson soon decided that the purchase of this land would bring great benefits to the United States and that he would not be performing his duty as President if he let the golden opportunity to acquire Louisiana pass by.

In 1803, the United States took possession of Louisiana. The purchase of Louisiana has been called "a great achievement", and indeed it was. Not only had it given the United States full control of the Mississippi River, but it had more than doubled the size of the United States!

TO THINK ABOUT: Use research books to answer the questions. Answer on a separate sheet of paper.
1. Explain why France did not want the Mississippi to fall into England's hands.
2. Why did President Jefferson want to avoid an alliance with England?
3. Explain how events in Europe made it possible for the United States to purchase Louisiana.
4. a. Who was Toussaint L'Ouverture?   b. Explain his importance in American history.
5. a. What is nepotism?   b. Give examples to show that Napoleon practiced nepotism.

          MILLIKEN PUBLISHING CO.   1

TROUBLE WITH BRITAIN

Napoleon's desire to control all of Europe had plunged the entire continent into war, and once again the United States was forced to declare its neutrality. Its attempts to remain neutral were not successful, however, for Britain began seizing American ships and impressing American seamen, while France took cargoes from American ships.

The worst insult to Americans occurred off the coast of Virginia in 1807. The United States frigate *Chesapeake* was ordered to stop by the *Leopard*, a British warship. The *Leopard* then opened fire, killing three men and wounding eighteen others. A British searching party then came aboard and removed four alleged deserters. Americans were aroused as they had not been since the XYZ Affair. Jefferson immediately issued a proclamation forbidding British ships to enter American waters.

President Jefferson wanted to avoid trouble with both countries, and, in an attempt to scare England and France into changing their policies, the Embargo Act was passed in 1807. This law said that American ships could not sail to any foreign port.

The law was a disaster from the beginning, however, for it almost ruined the American economy. Merchandise spoiled in warehouses, thousands of workers in shipping ports were out of work, farmers and trappers lost markets for their products, and merchants and shipowners were losing money. Many shipowners defied the law and smuggled goods out of the country and returned with contraband European goods.

In 1809, the Embargo Act was repealed and a law prohibiting trade only with France and England was passed, but both countries continued to prey on American ships.

Although the United States had equal grievances against both England and France, events seemed to be forcing a serious quarrel with Britain. Many settlers were moving west of the Alleghenies into land belonging to the Indians. In 1811, Chief Tecumseh, leader of the Shawnees, and his brother, the Prophet, united the tribes and formed the Tecumseh Confederation. The purpose of this confederation was to prevent the Americans from taking their hunting grounds. Tecumseh and the Prophet set up their headquarters on the Wabash River, near Tippecanoe Creek. While Tecumseh was in the South urging the Creek and the Cherokees to join the confederacy, the Prophet attacked a force of Americans led by William Henry Harrison, the governor of the Indiana Territory. The Indians were beaten back and abandoned their headquarters, which Harrison burned. Tecumseh fled to the British in Canada.

Americans accused the British of encouraging Tecumseh and inciting the Indians on the frontier. In their bitter feelings against England, people forgot that the Indians were simply trying to hold on to land that had been theirs for years!

In Congress there were a number of men who believed in the doctrine of manifest destiny. That is, they believed that it was their divine destiny to inhabit a continental empire that stretched from coast to coast. Their immediate objective was Canada, which was owned by England, and Florida, which belonged to Spain, England's ally. These men began to urge a war with Britain to gain more territory. These warlike enthusiasts were called the "War Hawks".

In Congress one word was heard almost constantly—Canada!

TO THINK ABOUT: Answer these questions fully on a separate sheet of paper.

1. Why did the United States have a difficult time trying to remain neutral in the quarrel between England and France?

2. a. Explain the theory of manifest destiny.
   b. Could this theory have been applied to Canada and Mexico? Explain your answer.

3. a. Why are those who advocate war called "hawks"? b. Why are opponents of war called "doves"?

4. Why was the Embargo Act not a workable solution to the problems with France and England?

5. Imagine that you are Chief Tecumseh. Prepare a speech explaining why you formed the Tecumseh Federation and urging tribes to join.

2

AN UNPOPULAR WAR

The most prominent War Hawks were John C. Calhoun of South Carolina, Henry Clay of Kentucky, and Felix Grundy of Tennessee. The War Hawks swept into power in the congressional election of 1810, and when Congress convened in 1811, Henry Clay was elected Speaker of the House. He, in turn, appinted other War Hawks to key positions on important Congressional committees. The War Hawks, who were all fiery orators, pounded at the idea of going to war. They knew that a war of expansion would not be popular, so they used the issues of impressment and harm to American trade to influence public opinion in favor of a war.

President Madison, pressured by the War Hawks, sent Congress a message in which he recommended that Congress declare war on Great Britain. Madison also included in his message the reasons for this recommendation; they were impressment (over six thousand cases over a three-year period), violation of American rights at sea, the blockade of American ports, the British interference with American commerce, and the encouragement of Indian uprisings.

In response to Madison's recommendation that action be taken, Congress declared war on Great Britain in June, 1812.

From the beginning, the War of 1812 was a mistake. It never really needed to happen. Only two days before Congress declared war, the British Parliament had agreed to discontinue the policies of seizure and impressment. Unfortunately there was no way for Congress to learn of the action of Parliament.

The United States was poorly prepared to fight a war. Its army and navy were pitifully small. The military leaders, for the most part, were old, incompetent, or inexperienced. The Secretary of War, William Eustis, was a likable physician who unfortunately knew very little about military matters. The senior officer of the army, Major General Henry Dearborn, was senile and inexperienced. Another military leader who contributed little to military success was Brigadier General William Hull, commander of the key post of Detroit. Only a few able leaders emerged from this second major conflict with Britain.

Congress had declared war but found that it could not provide the money to finance the war.

The most serious obstacle to the war was the attitude of the American people. There were violent disagreements concerning the war. Although the South and the West favored the war, the New England States were united in their opposition to the war. New England claimed that the war was ruining their economy, and many New Englanders were afraid of the naval power of the British and their ability to bombard New England's port cities and towns.

Opposition to the war was led by the Federalists of New England, who made it a political issue. In December, 1814, the Federalists met in Hartford, Connecticut, to formally declare their opposition to the war. Representatives of the New England states attended the Hartford Convention, which proposed seven amendments to the Constitution, most of which would have protected New England's sectional interests against the South and the West. One of these resolutions declared that a state must be allowed to resist any law which it believed interfered with the liberties of its people. The Hartford Convention even hinted at the possibility of secession. This was the first time that the idea of a state withdrawing from the Union had been considered. The war ended before the Hartford Convention could take any real action, but because its members were considered unpatriotic by the rest of the country, the Hartford Convention did much to contribute to the death of the Federalist party.

The events of this war were also to have a lasting effect on the relations of the United States with its neighbor to the north, Canada. Canadians rightfully resented the attempts of the United States to annex their land. The actions of the United States during this period of its history caused hard feelings in Canada which lasted many years.

MILLIKEN PUBLISHING CO.

ACTIVITY SHEET

I. HISTORY WORDS TO KNOW: Place the following words and expressions on your vocabulary sheet. Define or explain each as it is used in this history book.

ceded   frigate   negotiations   alleged   depleted   proclamation   nepotism

neutrality   impress   right of deposit   grievances   confederation   embargo   doctrine

inciting   repealed   manifest destiny   advocate   blockade   secession   contraband   annex

II. TO THINK ABOUT: Answer each of the following questions in the space provided.

1. a. List three weaknesses of the United States at the beginning of the War of 1812.

_____

_____

   b. Explain which of these weaknesses you consider to be the most serious.

_____

_____

2. Explain why the New England states opposed the war.

_____

_____

_____

3. What was the purpose of the Hartford Convention?

_____

_____

4. a. What is meant by secession?

_____

   b. Why would secession be a dangerous thing?

_____

_____

   c. What resulted when secession was tried later in United States history?

_____

5. Describe the attitude of most Canadians toward the War of 1812.

_____

_____

III. RESEARCH TOPICS: Use reference books, biographies, etc., to make reports on any or all of the following subjects.

Toussaint L'Ouverture   Tecumseh   The Hartford Convention   The Prophet   John C. Calhoun
Henry Clay   William Eustis   Henry Dearborn   Talleyrand   William Hull

THE WAR OF 1812-I

The War of 1812 began with one of several attempts to conquer Canada. The Americans had made elaborate plans to conquer Canada, but every one of these plans failed because of the lack of teamwork among the American fighting units, continual quarrels between commanding officers, and the refusal of the state militias to leave their own states.

On August 16, 1812, the first of a series of disasters occurred. The British forced Governor William Hull to surrender Detroit without firing a shot. Hull was court-martialed as a coward and sentenced to death. President Madison, pardoned the aged man because he had been a valuable officer in the American Revolution.

In the spring of 1813, the Americans incurred the wrath of the British and Canadians alike when they entered Canada and burned several towns, including York (Toronto), the capital city. On October 5, 1813, General William Henry Harrison routed a large British force and their Indian allies in the Battle of the Thames. The Indian leader, Tecumseh, was killed in the battle, and the Indian menace in the Northwest Territory was removed once and for all.

Much of the American success on the Canadian border was due to the naval battles fought on the Great Lakes. Commodore Oliver Hazard Perry won stunning victories against the British. On September, 10, 1813, after the fierce Battle of Lake Erie at Put-in-Bay, Perry reported to the President, "We have met the enemy and they are ours."

One of the most brilliant naval achievements of the war took place on Lake Champlain. Thomas Macdonough, commander of the American ships on Lake Champlain, skillfully outmaneuvered the entire British squadron, causing every British ship to sink or surrender. British troops in the area quickly withdrew, leaving the Americans in full command of Lake Champlain.

The last major battle on the Canadian border was fought at Lundy's Lane near Fort Niagara. General Winfield Scott and General Jacob Brown fought and defeated a stronger British force but were unable to follow up their victories, and the Battle of Lundy's Lane ended in a stalemate.

Unsuccessful in their attempts to gain a foothold inside the northern borders of the United States, the British began to raid and burn cities on the Atlantic coast. On August 24, 1814, the British invaded Washington, D. C. Two days before the enemy arrived, President Madison left the capital to join the military leaders in the Chesapeake Bay area. His wife Dolley remained in Washington, determined to save the nation's official documents and papers and valuable art treasures. She loaded the nation's valuables in a wagon and fled to the Virginia woods as the British entered the city and set fire to the White House, the Capitol, and other government buildings.

The British then sailed up Chesapeake Bay to attack the city of Baltimore, Maryland. The British fleet bombarded Fort McHenry from the sea, because they were unable to capture the fort by land. A young American lawyer named Francis Scott Key found himself aboard the British flagship to discuss an exchange of prisoners. When the bombardment began, Key was not allowed to leave the ship. He watched anxiously through the night as the shelling of the fort continued. In "the dawn's early light," Key saw the American flag still proudly flying over Fort McHenry. Key set down his feelings in a poem. "The Star-Spangled Banner" was later adopted as the national anthem.

MATCHING: Before each man's name in Column A, write the letter of the battle from Column B with which he is most closely associated.

A.

_____1. William Hull   _____2. Oliver Perry   _____3. Winfield Scott

_____4. Thomas   _____5. Francis   _____6. William Henry
          Macdonough   Scott Key   Harrison

B.

a. Lundy's Lane   d. The Thames
b. Lake Champlain e. Lake Erie
c. Fort McHenry

THE WAR OF 1812—II

For a short time, the Americans proved to be superior on the sea. The American ships were better built, better manned, and better armed than the British ships. The American frigates, the *President*, the *United States*, and the *Constitution* achieved some brilliant naval victories. The pride of the American fleet was the *Constitution*, called *Old Ironsides* because of her seemingly impenetrable hull. On August 19, 1812, the *Constitution* met the British frigate, the *Guerriére*, about 750 miles east of Boston. After a severe battle, the *Constitution* reduced the *Guerriére* to a floating wreck. It was during this battle that the *Constitution* received her nickname, *Old Ironsides*. The *Constitution* sank the British *Java* off the coast of Brazil on December 29, 1812. The *Constitution's* victories gave Americans new hope at a low point in the war, and the ship became a symbol of the fighting spirit of the American navy.

On June 1, 1813, the *Chesapeake* was defeated off the coast of Boston by the British *Shannon*. The American commander, Captain James Lawrence, was a brave but inexperienced seaman who refused to admit defeat. Lawrence was mortally wounded in the battle and as the British boarded his vessel, his dying words were, "Don't give up the ship!"

In spite of some brilliant victories by individual American ships, the British navy continued to rule the waves. In time the superior numbers of British warships were able to force the Americans into port and blockade them. The war at sea was continued by privateers, armed merchant ships which were chartered by the government to capture or destroy British vessels.

The campaigns in the South were dominated by one man—Andrew Jackson. On March 27, 1814, Jackson defeated the Creek Indians at Horseshoe Bend in the Mississippi Territory, thereby breaking the power of the Creeks and forcing them to give up all their land claims in Alabama. Jackson then marched into Spanish East Florida and, in effect, captured it. The United States did not press his conquest, however, and troops were not sent to occupy it.

The final battle of the war, like the war itself, was a mistake. The Battle of New Orleans was fought <u>after</u> the peace treaty had been signed. If there had been speedy communication, this battle might have been prevented, but Jackson did not know that a peace treaty had been signed in December. On January 8, 1815, the Americans, under the command of Andrew Jackson, and their French allies, under the command of the pirate, Jean Lafitte, were attacked by a British force of more than 8,000 men. The British laughed at the Americans who were entrenched behind bales of cotton, but in less than twenty minutes, Jackson's riflemen and Lafitte's pirates had killed more than two thousand British soldiers. Only eight of Jackson's force lost their lives in that needless battle, and only thirteen were wounded. Jackson was proclaimed a national hero and was called "the hero of New Orleans."

Both the Americans and the British were eager to bring the war to an end. On December 24, 1814, the Treaty of Ghent was signed. The peace treaty signed at Ghent, Belgium, returned conditions to their pre-war status. Neither side had gained anything.

One of the American officials best summed up the treaty and the war in one sentence—"We have gained nothing but peace."

TO THINK ABOUT: Use research books to answer these questions fully on a separate sheet of paper.

1. Name some of the items that Dolley Madison was able to save.
2. Tell the complete story of the writing of "The Star-Spangled Banner" and its adoption as the national anthem of the United States.
3. For years people have talked about changing the national anthem. Why do some want it changed?
4. Explain how the British were able to defeat the American fleet when the Americans were thought to have better ships, better men, and better equipment.
5. Was it right for the United States to use pirates in the war? Explain your answer.
6. Explain the statement, "We have gained nothing but peace."

Name _____ Date _____

A CROSSWORD PUZZLE

```
            L
       1    O
  9         U              10
       3    I
            S
       6    I                    5
            A
  2         N              7
            A
```

A. Complete the word puzzle
   using the word clues given below.

1. New _____, an important river port.

2. _____, advisor to Napoleon.

3. The Treaty of _____ returned Louisiana to France.

4. James _____, sent to France to purchase New Orleans.

5. _____ of 6. _____, permission to unload goods at New Orleans.

7. President _____ made the Louisiana Purchase.

8. Santo _____, site of slave uprising.

9. Toussaint _____, leader of slave uprising.

10. _____, original owner of Louisiana.

B. Complete these statements to make them true.

11. The _____ forbade any American ship to sail for a foreign port.

12. The doctrine of _____ said that the United States had to expand
    to its natural boundaries.

13. _____ of South Carolina was a leader of the War Hawks.

14. _____ commanded the American Navy on the Great Lakes.

15. The _____ protested the War of 1812.

16. _____ saved many valuable documents from the flames at
    Washington, D.C.

17. The attack on Fort _____ inspired the Star Spangled Banner.

18. The Battle of New Orleans was won by General _____.

19. _____ was a French pirate who aided the Americans at New
    Orleans.

20. The _____ ended the War of 1812.

A YOUNG NATION DEVELOPS

MILLIKEN PUBLISHING CO.

THE MONROE DOCTRINE

As the War of 1812 ended, the United States was able to realize several important results of this conflict. First, there was a new sense of national spirit or nationalism. The various sections of the country had forgotten their differences and had worked together. Secondly, the United States had begun to build its own manufacturing industry. It no longer relied on England for manufactured goods. Finally, two new leaders emerged as a result of the war. Both men had been heroes in the war. William Henry Harrison had fought on the Canadian border, and Andrew Jackson was the hero of the Battle of New Orleans.

With the conclusion of the War of 1812, the United States had to consider its place in the world. It had made a serious blunder in attacking Canada. The Canadians believed that they had been attacked for no reason. The wounds of this conflict took many years to heal.

The countries of Europe, on the other hand, looked at the United States with new respect. Americans had gone to war a second time to defend themselves. The European countries decided that it would be best to leave the United States alone.

Inspired by the success of the American Revolution, the colonies of Spain and Portugal had fought for and won their independence. One by one the countries of Mexico, Central America, and South America declared themselves independent republics. Canada alone chose the path of peaceful self-determination within the British Commonwealth.

Spain and Portugal were anxious to reclaim their colonies. England wanted the newly-formed republics to remain free so that she could trade freely with them. In the Pacific Northwest, Russia was eagerly pressing her land claims from Alaska to northern California.

Although the United States was not directly involved in these land claims, it recognized that the presence of European powers in the Western Hemisphere could represent a serious and constant danger to its security. The Latin American republics were weak and unable to defend themselves. After centuries of Spanish domination, the ideas of democracy did not flourish. There were constant internal power struggles which kept the republics weak and disunited.

Recognizing this, President James Monroe took a bold step in 1923. He proposed to the Congress the Monroe Doctrine, which was to become the basis of United States foreign policy. In effect, the Monroe Doctrine made the United States the protector of the Western Hemisphere. It provided that (1) the United States would consider European interference with any government in the Americas as an aggressive and unfriendly act; (2) no new colonies were to be established in this hemisphere; (3) the United States would not attempt to interefere with European affairs as long as the sovereignty of the Americas was not violated; (4) the United States had, in effect, issued a second declaration of independence covering all of the Western Hemisphere. Assuming the role of protector, the United States warned Europe to keep out. The War of 1812 had proved that the young nation was strong enough to back up its words. The Monroe Doctrine enabled the countries of the Americas to follow their own destinies without the interference of the European powers.

TO THINK ABOUT: Answer these questions fully on a separate sheet of paper.
1. a. Why can nationalism be considered an advantage to a country?
   b. Do you think it is possible for a country to have too much nationalism? Explain.
2. Explain how the War of 1812 forced the United States to develop its own manufacturing and industry.
3. Why did the United States think it had to protect the other countries of the Western Hemisphere?
4. What were the provisions of the Monroe Doctrine?
5. Can you find out how the United States did not always "practice what it preached" in regard to the Latin American countries?

A YOUNG NATION DEVELOPS

MILLIKEN PUBLISHING CO.

TRADE AND MANUFACTURING

How did the people of the United States make a living? As you know, even from colonial times most of the people made their living on farms. In the Northeast this was very difficult. In New England, especially, the land was not suitable for large-scale agriculture. Gradually the people of New England, as well as Pennsylvania, New York, and New Jersey turned to other means of earning money. The Northeast became the center of American trade and manufacturing.

The Revolutionary War dealt a serious blow to this section of the country. Most American ships had been captured or sunk. Many sailors had been killed, and many others gave up the sea for the life of frontier pioneers. The two largest markets were now closed to the United States-Great Britain and the West Indies.

Using Yankee determination and ingenuity, the Americans resolved to find new markets for their goods. The Yankee traders first turned their eyes to the East—to the Orient, an untapped market. Ships such as the *Empress of China* and the *Columbia*, captained by Robert Gray, sailed around Cape Horn and opened the doors to China.

Gray stopped on the Oregon coast to take on furs which he acquired from the Oregon Indians, and then proceeded to China, where he traded the furs for spices, silk, jade, and other Oriental products. Gray returned to the east coast of the United States by sailing around Africa.

Other traders went to the Baltic Sea to open trade with Russia, Denmark, and Sweden. Still others went to the Mediterranean area.

The Mediterranean trade was hampered by the Barbary pirates who controlled the Barbary Coast—Tripoli, Tunis, Algeria, and Morocco. These pirates would seize foreign ships and their crews and hold them for ransom. Most countries paid tributes to the pirates for the right to sail the Mediterranean. The United States did the same. In 1795, the United States agreed to pay Algeria an annual sum of money. A few years later the same agreement was made with Tripoli. The ruler of Tropoli did not like the treaty and in 1801 he declared war on the United States. Jefferson hoped to maintain peace, but the thought of

American seamen being chained, branded, and sold into Moorish slavery prompted him to use force against Tripoli. American warships sailed for North Africa to do battle with the pirates. Stephen Decatur, a young lieutenant, distinguished himself in an assault on the port of Tripoli. The United States Marines were particularly effective in the campaign. The war was concluded with an exchange of prisoners and a payment of sixty thousand dollars to ransom the captured ships and crews. The United States was the first country to stand up to the pirates. The action against Tripoli gave the United States a new dignity and sense of accomplishment.

It seemed then that the Northeast was well established as a major trade and manufacturing center. The War of 1812 brought an abrupt halt to the progress.

REVIEW: Answer these questions fully on a separate sheet of paper.

1. Why did the Revolutionary War almost destroy the New England economy?
2. a. What new markets were opened by the Yankee traders?

   b. Why did the traders choose these countries?
3. In what way did the Barbary pirates threaten the development of the U.S. trade?
4. What was the real importance of the Marine assault on Tripoli?
5. In a research book try to discover how the United States Marines came to be known as "leathernecks".

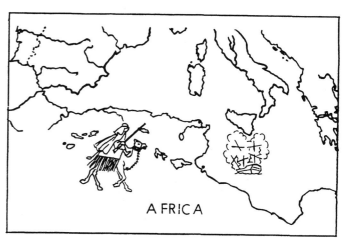

AFRICA

SHIPPING AND WHALING

As the merchant ships were sailing the seas and returning with cargoes of hemp, palm oil, coffee, spices, and hides, other ships and men were off on even more dangerous voyages. Great fleets of fishing vessels set sail from the New England ports. The most important of these fishing vessels were the whalers. Whale oil was in great demand to light the lamps of America. It was the common lighting oil until the 1860's when kerosene came into use. Whalebone, too, was a profitable product which had many uses. Ambergris, a waxy substance found in sperm whales, was highly prized by the makers of perfume. This substance gives a lingering quality to the scent of the perfume.

Whaling was a time-consuming and lonely occupation. Frequently the sailors on a whaler were gone for two or three years at a time. The whales were killed and processed at sea. Great kettles on board ship were used to render the whale blubber into oil which was stored in huge casks in the ship's hold. The rewards of this hard life were great. Many young sailors not much older than teenagers chose the life of a whaler and were able to retire as wealthy men before they were forty.

The trading ships, fishing boats, and whaling vessels helped to restore the United States to a prominent place in the economic structure of the world.

Then in 1812 catastrophe struck. The War of 1812 and the Embargo Act which preceded it reduced the trade of the United States. Warehouses overflowed with goods which could not be exported; sailors walked the piers idly, unable to practice the only trade they knew; American ships rotted in the harbors. It is little wonder that the people of the Northeast were opposed to the War of 1812, which threatened to destroy them.

At the conclusion of the war, the Yankee sea captains once more determined to claim their share of the world's trade.

In the 1840's a new American vessel appeared on the seas. Pioneered by men like Donald McKay, the clipper ship made America the leader in ocean shipping once more. These clipper

THE *FLYING CLOUD*

ships were long, slender vessels with tremendous sails which gave them great speed over long distances. The *Flying Cloud*, the most famous clipper ship, could "round the horn" from New York to San Francisco in less than ninety days.

For almost twenty years, the clipper ships ruled the seas, but their dominance was to come to an end with the appearance of the ocean-going steamship. The English pioneered these iron boats which would use steam to propel them, thus eliminating the need for fair winds. The Americans considered the stubby, smoke-belching, iron boxes to be just an ugly fad which would soon pass. They stubbornly clung to the sleek, speedy clipper ships. It was a serious error which cost them the control of the seas. In time the steamship became the new pride of the ocean, and the clipper ships became only a memory.

REVIEW: Answer these questions fully on a separate sheet of paper.

1. Explain how whales were an important part of the United States' economy.
2. How did the War of 1812 destroy the fishing and shipping industries?
3. a. Do you think smuggling was a traitorous act? b. Explain your answer.
4. How did Donald McKay make the United States the ruler of the seas?
5. Why did the United States lose its superiority on the seas?
6. a. What were the advantages of the clipper ship?
   b. What were the advantages of the ocean steamship?
7. Explain the expression "'round the horn."

 -MILLIKEN PUBLISHING CO.

THE INDUSTRIAL REVOLUTION

In the early 1760's, the British textile industry still relied on hand labor to spin single threads on a spinning wheel and to weave the threads on hand looms. This was also the method used in the new American textile industry. In 1764, a remarkable series of events were put in motion. This was the beginning of the Industrial Revolution, which introduced the use of power machines and the factory system to the textile industry.

James Hargreaves, a weaver with little formal education, was fascinated by an overturned spinning wheel which continued to spin. Working on the idea, he invented an eight spindle spinner which he called the *spinning jenny*, in honor of his wife. The local spinners were so afraid that the spinning jenny would cause them to lose their jobs that they broke into Hargreave's house and destroyed the machine. The spinning jenny was soon perfected by Richard Arkwright. Arkwright's machine handled eighty spindles at once. Yarn was now being produced so rapidly that the looms could not handle it. In 1785 Edmund Cartwright invented a power loom which could handle the increased yarn production.

Since the new machinery required power, the first mills were located near swiftly moving streams which provided the power by means of paddle wheels. With the invention of the first practical steam engine by James Watt in the late 1700's, it was no longer necessary to rely on streams for power. The mills were moved to towns where there was a large labor force.

Richard Arkwright is credited with putting the spinning jennies and power looms in the same building and creating the first textile factory in England.

Since England alone controlled these machines, she had a monopoly on fairly inexpensive cotton and woolen goods. The United States, which still relied on hand spinning and weaving, could not compete with the English manufacturers.

Parliament understood the value of the factories and did not intend to share the machines with the outside world. In 1774 and again in 1781, severe laws were passed to prohibit the exportation of any textile machines or any plans, models, or diagrams of the machines. People who were familiar with the machines were discouraged from leaving the country. In this way Parliament hoped to maintain the textile monopoly as part of England's policy of mercantilism.

The invention of power machines soon brought improvements in the English mining, iron, and steel industries, as well as in the textile mills and factories.

The Industrial Revolution had changed the industrial face of a nation. No longer were the spinners and weavers independent craftsmen. They were now employees in factories owned by someone else, working on machines which they did not own. No longer would manufacturing have its original meaning—"made by hand". The Industrial Revolution was to bring about more far-reaching effects than any warlike revolution had ever done.

I. TO THINK ABOUT: Answer these questions fully on a separate sheet of paper.

1. a. What is mercantilism?
   b. Explain how a textile monopoly would help the British theory of mercantilism.
2. How would you define the Industrial Revolution?
3. Explain the contribution made by each of the following men to the Industrial Revolution.
   a. James Hargreaves b. Richard Arkwright c. Edmund Cartwright d. James Watt e. Samuel Crompton

II. RESEARCH QUESTIONS: Use research books to answer the following questions.

1. a. What is the origin of each of the following words.? a. sincerely b. hallmark
   b. What do sincerely and hallmark mean today?
2. a. How were the medieval guilds like our present-day labor unions?
   b. How were they different?
3. **What was** Crompton's "mule"?

REVIEW

I. Identify each man from the description given. Write his name in the space provided.

1. _____ I am an American general who became a hero in the War of 1812. I fought along the Canadian border.

2. _____ I am an American president who declared that the United States would protect the rights of all the Americans.

3. _____ I am the American officer who led an assault against the Tripoli pirates.

4. _____ I am the American commander who won the Battle of New Orleans.

5. _____ I am an American sea captain who helped open trade with China.

6. _____ I am the ship designer who was largely responsible for developing the clipper ship.

7. _____ I am an American who invented a spinning device and named it after my wife.

8. _____ I invented the first practical power loom.

9. _____ I opened the first textile factory and also improved on earlier power machines.

10. _____ I invented the device which made the Industrial Revolution possible.

II. Fill in each blank with the correct word from the list below.

11. _____, the change from hand-made goods to machine-made goods; the advent of power machines and the factory system.

12. _____, an early multiple thread spinning wheel.

13. _____, an early American ships to trade with the Orient.

14. _____, a whale product used in the manufacture of perfume.

15. _____, one of the best known clipper ships.

16. _____, stated that Europe was to stay out of the Western Hemisphere and that the United States would not meddle in European affairs.

17. _____, one of the early American ships to trade with the Orient.

18. _____, an American trading ship captained by Robert Gray.

19. _____, the control of an industry, a product, etc., by a single person, group or country.

20. _____, the Monroe Doctrine proclaimed.

the *Empress of China*	sewing machine	whale oil
the *Columbia*	Industrial Revolution	1816
Monroe Doctrine	monotony	the *Flying Cloud*
Barbary Coast	1823	
ambergris	spinning jenny	monopoly 1824
	Baltic Sea	protective tariff steam engine

A YOUNG NATION DEVELOPS

MILLIKEN PUBLISHING CO.

MANUFACTURING IN AMERICA—I

Manufacturing had a very slow start in colonial America. Most of the population was involved in some form of agriculture. In New England, where the poor soil would not support large scale farming, some people turned to lumbering, shipping, and fishing.

In almost every community, there could be found men who made furniture and household supplies. Carpenters, blacksmiths, and tanners also operated in most towns. Spinning wheels and looms were found in most homes. The manufacturing that was done was usually an individual matter with most articles being made by an individual in his own home for the use of his family.

Skilled artisans began to produce extra items for their neighbors, and in this way, small businesses were begun. These craftsmen worked from their own homes and were responsible for the entire product from its beginning to its completion.

In New England and some of the middle colonies the people began to do their manufacturing in the small towns that developed. In the South, the plantations tended to be self-sufficient, which did not contribute to the development of towns as centers of manufacturing.

During the colonial period, England was very careful to keep colonial manufacturing at a minimum. It was important for England's mercantilism that the colonies bought more than they sold. This could best be accomplished by keeping the colonies agricultural rather than industrial.

As the Revolutionary War approached, it was clear that the states could no longer rely on England to supply manufactured goods. As a result, the states turned to manufacturing the goods which were needed. This was particularly true of iron, textiles, and ordnance. Great profits were made by New England in the newly developed industries.

After the war there was a bleak period for the infant colonial industries. England was once again willing to flood the market with cheap goods. In England the Industrial Revolution was making it impossible for the handmade American goods to compete.

Although the United States had won its political independence from Britain, it remained bound to the British as a source of cheap manufactured goods.

The manufacturing industry continued to creep along after the revolution but was unable to make much progress. The Embargo Acts almost destroyed what was left of the American industries.

Once again the industrial economy was saved by a war. The War of 1812 closed off the British flow of goods and the United States had to rely on domestic goods. After the war, the Northeast found itself on a sound footing. It began to expand and develop and the Industrial Revolution crossed the Atlantic with a new wave of English immigrants.

TO THINK ABOUT: Answer these questions fully on a separate sheet of paper.

1. Why did England not encourage the development of manufacturing in the colonies?
2. a. Use a dictionary to find out the differences in the meanings of these words: artist, artisan, laborer.
   b. Which word would best describe a carpenter of the colonial period?
   c. Which word would best describe a mill worker in an early factory?
3. a. What does self-sufficient mean?
   b. In what ways was a plantation like a medieval manor?
4. Explain why the early attempts at American manufacturing were limited to metal, ordnance, and textiles.
5. Explain this statement: "The United States had gained political independence but not economic independence from England."
6. Although the Northeast opposed the War of 1812, this war proved a blessing to them. Explain why.

MANUFACTURING IN AMERICA—II

As news concerning the new machines reached America, Americans determined to find ways to duplicate them. The manufacturers resorted to smuggling and copying until most of the successful English inventions had been duplicated in the United States.

As early as 1775, a spinning jenny patterned after the Hargreaves models was operating in Philadelphia. Two Scotch immigrants, Robert and Alexander Barr, were hired by the state of Massachusetts in 1786 to develop machines which would card, rope, and spin cotton and wool. Their machines were based on the Arkwright models.

Samuel Slater had worked in the mills in his native England. By the time he came to America to settle, he had memorized the designs of most of the machines. Slater settled in Pawtucket, Rhode Island, and built copies of these machines from memory. In 1789 he built a crude textile factory and later opened several more.

In 1814 Francis Lowell opened the first complete factory for the manufacture of raw cotton into cotton cloth. Lowell is also credited with introducing the power loom to the United States in his factory at Waltham, Massachusetts.

Although the introduction of machinery was tried in the South and West, it was the Northeast which developed as the manufacturing center of the United States. There were numerous rushing streams to supply water power. The farmland was poor, and people willingly left the land to work in factories. There were many ships to carry goods to foreign ports. When the transition was made from water power to steam, the Northeast found that there was ample lumber and coal to be used as fuel for the steam engines.

American inventors were directing their attention to producing new machines and to perfecting those which had been copied from the English models. Oliver Evans, James Ramsey, and John Fitch were three early inventors who contributed to the American Industrial Revolution.

It was now possible to spin and weave by machine, but the cloth still had to be sewn by hand. There was a desperate need for a machine that could sew. Elias Howe, a farmer turned factory worker, was skilled at making tools. He worked on the problem for many years, and in 1845 perfected a sewing machine. Howe's machine was slow in catching on, and many imitations of his design flooded the market. At this time Howe had difficulty getting a patent for his invention, and, as a result, received very little financial reward for his design. For many years Howe lived in poverty before his patent rights were settled, and he and his family became wealthy.

Howe's invention greatly helped the textile industry. Clothes made by the sewing machine were much cheaper to produce and could be sold for less than hand-sewn clothing.

The Industrial Revolution had come to the American shores and brought with it undreamed of changes.

TO THINK ABOUT: Answer these questions fully on a separate sheet of paper.

1. Tell the contributions of each of the following men to the American Industrial Revolution. a) Samuel Slater b) Elias Howe c) Francis Lowell d) Robert and Alexander Barr.
2. Give several reasons why manufacturing did not work well in the West and in the South.
3. Do you think it was ethical for American manufacturers to copy the designs of English machines? Explain your answer.
4. a. What is a patent? b. How is it used to protect an inventor? c. What is the purpose of a copyright?
5. The American Industrial Revolution brought about the era of mass production. Give several advantages of this type of manufacturing. b. Can you give any disadvantages of it?

HISTORY WORDS TO KNOW: Add these words and their definitions to your vocabulary list.

tanner   textile   economy   ordnance   immigrant   mass production

GOVERNMENT HELP

As the factory system developed in the United States, the general quality of the manufactured goods was poor. Consumers accepted these goods only when they could not get English goods, which were generally of a better quality. After the War of 1812 when the United States again began to trade with England, the American consumers wished to buy the imported goods which were less expensive, as well as better made. As a result of this foreign competition, American factory owners lost considerable amounts of money.

The manufacturers in the Northeast looked to the federal government for help. They requested that a tariff be placed on manufactured goods brought into the country. They argued that the government could use this tax money to help the country. They called it a protective tariff because it would protect the American industries from foreign competition.

How would this work? A foreign manufacturer would have to add the amount of the tax to the cost of his goods in order to make a profit. For example, a shirt originally priced to sell for five dollars might have a tariff tax of fifty cents placed on it. The shirt would then have to be sold for $5.50. The American manufacturers hoped to make the English goods cost as much or possibly more than American goods by using this tariff. In 1816, a protective tariff was placed on imported goods.

Many Americans did not like the idea of a protective tariff. Shipowners feared that England might boycott our goods causing them to lose cargoes. Southerners and Westerners were afraid that if the English lost too many sales, they would cut down on the raw materials, such as cotton, which they purchased from the South and the West. Most American consumers disliked the tariff because they felt that they were being forced to pay higher prices.

In fact, many people went so far as to claim that the tariff was a violation of the United States Constitution. They said that no state could be given preferential treatment over another (Article I, Section IX, Paragraph 6), and that the tariff was clearly designed to benefit the states of the industrial Northeast. They were, however, unable to take any legal action to successfully block the tariff.

The tariff worked and the manufacturers found themselves growing wealthy. As their wealth increased so did their political power. As they became more and more powerful, they began to demand that new and higher tariffs be imposed in an effort to even further reduce their competition. They were able to exert enough political pressure to get a higher tariff law passed in 1824, and an even higher one passed in 1828.

The government had gained a new source of revenue, and the Northeast was protected from foreign competition, but the tariff question caused many deep wounds in the South and in the West. As we will see later, these wounds were very slow to heal.

TO THINK ABOUT: Answer these questions fully on a separate sheet of paper.

1. Why were the English goods cheaper and usually better than domestic goods?
2. What is a protective tariff?
3. Although the Northeast wanted the tariff, other sections did not. Why?
4. A. Look up Article I, Section IX, Paragraph 6 of the United States Constitution. Explain what it says in your own words.
   B. Do you think that this part of the Constitution prohibits a tariff? Explain.
5. Explain how a tariff keeps United States money in the country and therefore benefits the entire country.
6. Explain this cartoon.

THE GOLDEN STAIRS

AMERICA CHANGES

Do you live in an urban or rural community? Until very recently, most Americans lived in rural areas, that is, in small towns or farm communities. Today the majority of the people of the United States live in large urban centers. This movement from farm to city began with the Industrial Revolution. When it was no longer necessary to place factories near running streams, they were built in towns which were closed to shipping routes. People moved to the towns from the farms to be near their work. Immigrants from Europe came directly to these factory towns, where they knew they could find jobs. As the numbers of workers increased, the towns grew and other services were introduced. Houses were built, stores and shops were opened, food had to be provided, warehouses were set up, and banks were established. The townspeople had to be provided with special services, such as doctors, lawyers, and policemen.

Living in a town provided people with many conveniences which they did not have on the farms. They had street lights and a city water supply. In their houses they had the new conveniences of oil lamps, cooking stoves, carpets, tin or ironware, and comfortable furniture. With so many people in a small area, there were more opportunities for social life in the churches, lodges, etc.

When a person started working in a factory, he found that his way of life changed. He lost much of his independence; he was no longer his own boss. He didn't own the tools with which he worked, and the items he made belonged to the factory owner. The factory worker soon lost the pride of accomplishment that a craftsman has when he completes an article by himself.

The factories themselves were not cheerful places. Usually they were large wooden buildings with poor light and poor ventilation. They were hot in the summer and bitter cold in the winter. There were no restrooms and no doctors or nurses in case of injury. The workers did not complain about these conditions, however.

Men, women, and even children as young as seven or eight worked side by side in the factory for twelve to fifteen hours a day, usually six days a week. The men were paid five dollars a week, the women two dollars, and the children one dollar. The pay was low but so was the cost of living. Most men hoped to save their money and eventually buy land in the West. The women hoped to marry and settle on a small farm somewhere.

Wages were kept low by a plentiful supply of immigrants who needed work. Workers who did ask for more money were fired. In time labor unions were formed to seek higher wages and shorter hours. In the 1830's there were many labor unions but they were disunited and weak. It was not until the 1860's that the labor movement grew strong enough to improve the working conditions in the factories.

As we have seen, America had begun to change, and life in the United States was becoming more complex.

REVIEW: Answer these questions fully on a separate sheet of paper.
1. In what ways did the Industrial Revolution contribute to the urbanization of the United States?
2. Name several special services which could be found in urban communities.
3. Describe conditions in the early factories.
4. A. What was the purpose of the first labor unions?
   B. How were labor unions like the guilds of early feudal times?
5. Today we hear a great deal about discrimination.
   A. What does this mean?
   B. Explain how the early factory owners practiced discrimination.

HISTORY WORDS TO KNOW: Put these words and their definitions on your vocabulary sheet.

| consumer | competition | tariff | preferential | urban |
| rural | ventilation | conveniences | discrimination | |

TEST AND REVIEW

A. Write True if the statement is true. Write False if the statement is false.

_____ 1. England wanted the colonies to develop their own industries.

_____ 2. The War of 1812 helped the United States to develop its own manufacturing.

_____ 3. The American manufacturers did not need the English machines.

_____ 4. Francis Lowell opened the first crude textile factory in 1814.

_____ 5. Unsuccessful attempts were made to use machinery in the West and South.

_____ 6. Oliver Evans, James Ramsey, and John Fitch were early American inventors.

_____ 7. Elias Howe invented the power-driven sewing machine.

_____ 8. After the War of 1812, Americans could not buy British-made goods.

_____ 9. The protective tariff was a great help to the Southern plantation owner.

_____ 10. Many people questioned the legality of the protective tariff.

_____ 11. The first protective tariff was passed in 1618.

_____ 12. After the Revolutionary War, most Americans lived in rural areas.

_____ 13. Labor unions were numerous but weak in the 1830's.

_____ 14. There was little job discrimination in the early factories since all workers were treated equally.

B. Answer the following by putting the letter of the correct answer in the space provided.

____ 15. Before the Industrial Revolution most goods were made in _____.
   a. the home   b. factories   c. union halls

____ 16. Francis Lowell is credited with introducing the _____ to the United States.
   a. power mill   b. power jenny   c. power loom

____ 17. Which section of the country benefitted most from manufacturing?
   a. the South   b. the West   c. the Northeast

____ 18. Who invented the sewing machine? a. Samuel Slater   b. Robert Barr   c. Elias Howe

____ 19. In what year was the first spinning jenny used in America? a. 1775   b. 1789   c. 1814

____ 20. Which of these was not a reason for the growth of early cities?
   a. immigrants   b. good farming   c. modern conveniences

____ 21. A tariff is placed on what type of goods? a. imported   b. exported   c. domestic

____ 22. Which group provided a cheap source of labor which tended to keep wages low in the early factories?   a. slaves   b. farmers   c. immigrants

Answer these questions fully on the back of this paper.

   23. Do you believe it was right for the early American manufacturers to copy the English machines and to smuggle the designs out of England? Explain your answer.

   24. Explain why Elias Howe and many other early inventors did not receive quick wealth from their inventions.

CHANGES IN THE SOUTH

From earliest colonial days, the South based its economy on agriculture. The most profitable crops were indigo, tobacco, and rice. Cotton was in demand, but it was a poor money crop since it involved the use of large numbers of workers to insure even a small profit. The cotton bolls contained many seeds which had to be separated from the fibers before the cotton fibers could be used. This work had to be done by hand, and it took a full day for a worker to clean a single pound of cotton.

The textile manufacturers of England and the United States demanded more and more cotton, but their needs could not be filled unless a machine to clean cotton could be found.

Eli Whitney changed the history of the South. Whitney had been interested in mechanics from his early childhood. He was a Connecticut school teacher who moved to Georgia in 1792. Friends there asked him to work on the problem of a mechanical device to clean cotton. In 1793 he perfected the *cotton gin*, which was a simple but effective device. Whitney's invention of the cotton gin made it possible for a worker to clean fifty pounds of cotton in a day compared to the one pound which could be done by hand.

Whitney applied for a patent on the gin, but it was slow in being granted. Others copied his idea, and he received practically nothing for his efforts. Later Whitney became a wealthy man by developing the idea of the mass production of firearms through the use of interchangeable parts.

The southern farmers were now able to produce the cotton that was in such great demand. Cotton became the most important crop in the South. To be profitable, cotton growing required two things: large amounts of land and plenty of cheap labor. As cotton became the "*king of crops*" in the South, the institution of slavery became a very necessary way of life to the plantation owners.

The soils of the original southern colonies (the **Old South**), Maryland, Virginia, North Carolina, South Carolina, and Georgia were not particularly good for cotton. The best cotton land was found in South Carolina and Georgia,

but this was soon depleted. When cotton is grown on the same soil year after year, the soil is ruined. The soil can be saved by rotating crops and using fertilizers to put minerals into the soil. Most plantation owners did not want to lose money by growing a crop other than cotton. Instead they preferred to raise as much cotton as possible, and when the soil was depleted, simply move on to new and better land.

This was possible for wealthy plantation owners who could afford to buy more land and to transfer their operations to new areas. Small farmers could only work the land until it was useless and then try to grow another money crop.

With the invention of the cotton gin, *King Cotton* became the most important thing to the South—and once again a King was to bring about a war!

REVIEW: Answer these on a separate sheet of paper.

1. Explain how the South was indirectly affected by the Industrial Revolution.
2. Eli Whitney is credited with creating the Cotton Kingdom. Explain why.
3. A. What other invention of Whitney's is considered very important? B. Explain why many people believe this is more important than the cotton gin.
4. Explain why cotton was hard on the soil.
5. A. Give this cartoon an appropriate title.

B. Explain the cartoon fully on a separate sheet of paper.

Name _____ Date _____

THE SOUTH EXPANDS

As the lands of the Old South became depleted, the cotton growers had to move to new lands. The migration moved in the direction of the **Lower South:** Alabama, Mississippi, and Louisiana. Some adventuresome planters even moved into Texas. The Lower South provided good land and rivers to transport the cotton.

As the land was carved into large plantations, there was an increasing demand for slaves. This need for more slaves created a problem. By law, no slaves could be brought into the United States after 1808. As a result, the market value of slaves increased greatly. The plantation owners of Virginia and the Carolinas were quick to turn the demand for slaves to their advantage. They sold the children of their slaves to the new plantation owners. Families were broken up with the probability that children would never see their parents again.

By the 1840's cotton had become the most important crop in the South. Other crops were still grown, however. Tobacco was grown in the Carolinas and Virginia. Rice was an important crop in South Carolina and Georgia. The raising of sugar cane was to become profitable in Louisiana.

Most of the cotton was grown in the Lower South. This area grew and developed much more rapidly than did the Old South.

Louisiana became a state in 1812, followed by Mississippi in 1817, and Alabama in 1819. Mobile, Alabama, and New Orleans, Louisiana, became the leading cities of this newly developed area.

The life and economy of the South were closely tied to cotton. The South was dependent on one thing to support its economy—cotton had to remain important. Anything that threatened the profit from cotton threatened the entire economic structure of the South.

One thing was a constant threat to the profits received from cotton: the loss of cheap slave labor. For many years slavery had been on the decline in the South. Influential people in the South declared that slavery was a barbaric and inhuman practice. In 1794 a representative in Congress stated, "Not a man in Georgia but

wishes there were no slaves; they are a curse to the country." It is interesting to note at this time that the price of a slave had fallen to about two hundred dollars.

By the time that cotton had become the dominant product in the South, the price of a good field hand had risen to as much as two thousand dollars. The attitude toward slavery had also changed. The spokesmen of the South were forced into a position of defending slavery as a good thing. Unable to base their position on just economic necessity, they tried to justify slavery as an institution that had historical backgrounds. They even went so far as to claim that slavery was acceptable even in the Bible. As the debate over slavery grew, the southerners found themselves being united in order to fight against outside pressures which were threatening them.

REVIEW: Answer these questions on a separate sheet of paper.

1. Why did New Orleans and Mobile develop as the two major cities of the Lower South?
2. Explain why it is not a good idea for a group to rely on only one product or industry for its economy.
3. What changed the attitude of the South toward slavery?
4. In a sense the defenders of slavery were hypocritical in their defense of slavery. Can you explain why?
5. In what way was slavery a unifying force in the South?
6. How would you answer the argument that slavery was a common and acceptable practice since it had existed all through history and even in biblical times?

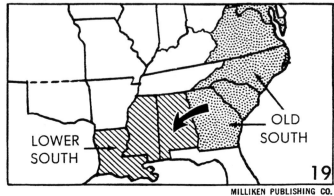

THE PLANTATION

In time the plantation owners became men of great wealth and power in the South, and they set the life style for the entire section. These wealthy and powerful men also became the spokesmen for the South in Congress.

The plantation system is one in which one crop is grown on large tracts of land with slave labor. A plantation consisting of several hundred acres of fields tended by fifty to a hundred slaves was considered to be a profitable operation.

Only the wealthy could afford large numbers of slaves, since the average slave cost between one and two thousand dollars. In a population of about five and a half million, fewer than ten thousand men in the South held fifty or more slaves. It is easy to see that most of the wealth of the South was concentrated in the hands of a relatively small number of men.

The work on a plantation centered around cotton. An overseer was in charge of this work and he saw to the operation of the plantation. An overseer was very much like a foreman.

The cotton was planted in the spring, tended all summer, and picked in the fall. After the cotton was picked, it was ginned (cleaned) and baled. The cotton bales, which were two or three feet wide and almost six feet tall, were then transported to the nearest river to be shipped by water to New Orleans or Mobile. From there the cotton was sent to the textile factories of the Northeast or to England.

The life of the plantation owner and his family centered around the large, comfortable main house. It was usually very ornate and richly furnished.

The master (plantation owner) supervised the management of the plantation and took care of the business accounts. He gave instructions to his overseer and saw to it that the slaves were instructed in their jobs.

The master's wife managed the house, supervised the household servants, and looked after the health and welfare of the slaves.

Sons of the plantation owner were taught to manage a plantation, while girls received instructions in the supervision of a household. There were many social activities for the children of a plantation owner. Parties, riding, hunting, and visiting were all a part of the full social life of these children. Frequently they were educated on the plantation by private tutors; sometimes they were sent to expensive private schools, often in England.

The slaves were usually field hands; some were chosen to work in the main house as servants. Others worked as carpenters and blacksmiths. Some very intelligent slaves were trained to act as doctors and nurses for the rest of the slaves. Most slaves, however, were kept illiterate so that they could be more easily controlled.

Slaves lived in crude log cabins. Their food consisted mostly of pork, corn meal, and molasses, plus a few vegetables which they were able to grow.

Some plantation owners never spent more than fifty dollars a year on each slave, and most masters spent less than half of that amount.

Although slaves were provided with living quarters, food, and clothing and were able to find some means of relaxation, they were deprived of the one thing they desperately wanted —their freedom.

REVIEW: Answer these questions on a separate sheet of paper.

1. If the plantation owners were in the minority, how was it possible for them to control the political life of the South?
2. a. Why was it considered desirable for slaves to be kept illiterate?
   b. Can you think of any modern examples of trying to keep people illiterate or educated in only a limited way?
3. In a research book, look up the encomienda system.
   a. What was it? b. In what ways did it resemble the plantation system?
4. a. In what ways was a serf on a manor like a slave?
   b. In what way was he different?
5. a. The black slave contributed a distinct form to American music. What was it?
   b. What purpose did this music serve for slaves?

THE OTHER SOUTH

Not all of the people who lived in the South lived on plantations. More than five million southerners had no part in the plantation system.

In the towns of the South the usual professions could be found. There were doctors, lawyers, tradesmen, shopkeepers, bankers, clergymen, and skilled workers. The wealthiest professional people frequently had one or two slaves who were considered more like family servants than slaves. Towns were slow to develop in the South since there was little interest in manufacturing. The major cities were those which could be used as shipping centers. The most important of these were Charleston, Savannah, Mobile, and New Orleans. In these cities, life was frequently stylish and formal. These cities were the cultural as well as the economic centers of the South.

The largest group of farmers in the South were the *small farmers*. These people owned and worked small plots of land which the plantation owners did not want. These farmers usually worked the land with the help of their families. They usually could not afford to have any slaves. By working very hard they were able to produce a few bales of cotton a year and the food on which they lived during the year. The small farmers accounted for about half of the cotton crop in the South. They lived in very humble houses with few conveniences. They had little chance for education or the social life of the plantation class.

Most of the small farmers dreamed of owning a plantation. By working hard and saving diligently, some of them were able to acquire more land, but only a very few were able to acquire vast plantations.

Another group of southerners lived completely apart from the rest of the South. These people were called the *mountain whites*. They has settled in the Appalachian Mountains and had kept themselves apart from the other southerners. They lived much like pioneer frontiersmen in crude log cabins furnished with handmade furniture. These mountain whites were a proud and self-sufficient group of people. They hunted wild game, fished in streams, and tended small gardens. They grew some corn which they made into corn whiskey. The whiskey was taken to town and sold or bartered for any essentials the mountain whites might need.

These mountain whites were not affected by the importance of cotton or the plantation system. They wanted to keep to themselves and to be left alone. They had no slaves and had no interest in slavery. Most of the mountain whites were descendants of immigrants from England, Scotland, and Wales. So great was their desire for privacy and isolation that for many years they preserved the accents, dialects, and culture of their ancestors in an almost pure state. Even today we can still find remnants of this mountain culture in parts of the Appalachian Mountains.

REVIEW: Answer these questions on a separate sheet of paper.
1. Why were there so few cities in the South?
2. Can you explain why the cities of the South followed the fashions of Europe and England more than northern cities did?
3. In what way were the mountain whites part of the South without being a part of it?
4. Many of the mountain whites were descendants of Scottish immigrants. Can you tell why these people would have chosen these regions in which to settle?
5. Although the southerners who lived in the cities did not have many slaves, they defended slavery. Can you think of two reasons why this was so?

HISTORY WORDS TO KNOW: Add these words and their definitions to your vocabulary list.

indigo	boll	textile	patent	firearm	interchangeable
the Old South	deplete	the Lower South		dominant	plantation system
overseer	dialect	barter	isolation		

TEST AND REVIEW

A. MATCHING:

Match the item from Column II with the item in Column I with which it is most closely associated. Put the letter of the correct item in the space provided.

COLUMN I

_____ 1. Eli Whitney

_____ 2. Old South

_____ 3. cotton

_____ 4. Lower South

_____ 5. 1808

_____ 6. Louisiana

_____ 7. Mobile, Alabama

_____ 8. southern economy

_____ 9. overseer

_____ 10. 1793

_____ 11. slaves

_____ 12. largest group in the South

_____ 13. mountain whites

_____ 14. barter

_____ 15. Georgia

_____ 16. patent

COLUMN II

A. Alabama, Louisana, Mississippi

B. cotton gin

C. sugar cane

D. small farmers

E. corn whiskey

F. Boston

G. Elias Howe

H. protects inventor

I. soil depletion

J. shipping center

K. King Cotton

L. foreman

M. illiterate

N. no slaves could be brought in

O. Appalachians

P. Alleghenies

Q. mass production

R. rice

S. Maryland, Virginia, Carolinas, Georgia

B. WHO AM I?

17. I am hired to run a plantation. It is my job to see that the slaves do their work and that everything runs smoothly. I am _____.

18. My main task is to run the mansion and to instruct the household slaves. I also look after the health and welfare of the slaves. I am _____.

19. My ancestors came from Scotland and I live very much like they did. I do not like to have much contact with the outside world. I am _____.

20. I work on a plantation in the fields. I live in a log cabin and have very few comforts. I am

SECTIONALISM—I

As the economy of the country developed, the North and South began to develop a number of striking differences. As we have already seen, the North turned to manufacturing, trade, and business. The South remained an agricultural region, relying exclusively on cotton to maintain its economy. There were more cities in the North, and most of the railroads had been built to connect the northern cities.

One of the major differences between the two sections was the question of slavery. Slavery had never been profitable in the North. The farms were too small to require the use of slaves, and the attempts to use slaves in the factories had proven disastrous. For the most part, the slaves could not be trained to use the machinery. If for some reason the factory had to close down, the owner still had to provide for the slaves.

The feeling against slavery was strong in the North, and by the early 1800's the North had freed its slaves. Freed slaves were called freedmen and were supposed to have the rights of a citizen. In most instances this was not true, even in the North. The boundary line between the slave and the free states was the Mason and Dixon Line which was drawn to mark the boundary between Maryland and Pennsylvania.

Before 1793 the feeling against slavery was not confined to the North. Many early southern leaders disliked the institution of slavery. George Washington hoped to see the end of slavery. At his death his slaves were freed. Both Patrick Henry and Thomas Jefferson maintained that slavery violated the ideas in the Declaration of Independence. Jefferson advanced a plan to free the slaves and return them to Africa. The Republic of Liberia in Africa was founded by former slaves. It's capital was named Monrovia in honor of President James Monroe.

Slavery was in integral part of the southern economy, and the South had to defend "their" institution against the growing opposition from the North. The northern opposition was solidified by the efforts of the abolitionists, who wanted all slavery ended at once.

The South began to unite against these attacks. John C. Calhoun defended slavery as a southern right. Southern churches which had once doubted slavery now defended it. Many denominations split into northern and southern branches over the slavery issue.

The South claimed that slavery was really better for the slave since all of his needs were taken care of by the slave owner. Southerners maintained that the slaves could not provide for themselves since they were uneducated. They failed to state that it was the slave owner who denied an education to the slaves.

REVIEW: Answer these questions on a separate sheet of paper.

1. What were the economic differences between the North and the South?
2. Why was slavery not profitable in the North?
3. Name the early leaders who were against slavery.
4. a. Who was the spokesman for the cause of slavery?
   b. In what other major period of United States history did this man play an important part?
5. a. Why were freedmen considered a threat to the workers in the North?
   b. What other groups of workers were considered threats to these workers? c. Why?

6. Explain this cartoon.

ONLY THE NAMES HAVE BEEN CHANGED

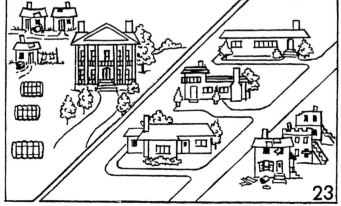

23

MILLIKEN PUBLISHING CO.

Name _____ Date _____

SECTIONALISM-II

The original disagreement between the North and the South was economic. The difference grew as the North demanded the protective tariff. When the tariff threatened to cut down on the English manufacturing, the South became alarmed. The South was bound to England by a cotton thread. The northern tariff threatened to break that thread.

In the end, however, it was the question of slavery that made the most damaging divisions between the two sections of the country. As one southern leader spoke, he seemed to be making a prophecy that was all too soon to come true.

He said, "Rather than yield our dearest rights and privileges—we should see the United States scattered to the four winds."

As the rivalry between these two sections was developing, a third section was working on its own problems. The frontier and the West had little interest in the economics of the North or the slavery of the South. The West was concerned with two things only: the availability of cheap land and the extension of good roads to the frontier. As the years passed, the questions of slavery drew the West into the growing disagreement between the North and the South.

REVIEW: Answer these questions on a separate sheet of paper.

1. a. What two issues were most important to the frontier West? b. Why?
2. Why would the West have to be drawn into the slavery question?
3. a. How do you think most Westerners would feel about the question of slavery? b. Why?
4. Study the chart below. Make one like it to show what the West wanted. Give your chart a title and label it.
5. On the map below color the North red, the South green, and the West yellow.

THE NORTH AND SOUTH DISAGREE

The North Wanted: **The South Wanted:**

High tariffs   Low tariffs

To close the West   To open the West

To abolish slavery   To keep slavery

A YOUNG NATION DEVELOPS

MILLIKEN PUBLISHING CO.

THE ABOLITIONISTS

The anti-slavery forces had many different ideas about ending slavery. They agreed only that slavery had to be abolished. These abolitionists became loosely organized in order to bring an end to the institution of slavery.

The earliest organized opposition to slavery came from the Quakers, who held that all men were equal before God and that no man could hold himself superior to another. Benjamin Franklin freed the slaves that he had owned. Benjamin Lundy, a Quaker living in Ohio, organized the Union Humane Society to help blacks. He proposed re-settlement outside the United States for free blacks. He also established one of the early abolitionist newspapers.

William Lloyd Garrison published *The Liberator*, probably the most successful anti-slavery publication of that period. Garrison believed in ending slavery at any cost, and many Southerners felt that his writings were responsible for such events as Nat Turner's slave revolt. Garrison wrote at a time when slavery was also coming under attack in foreign lands. In 1829 Mexico had abolished slavery and in 1833 England outlawed the practice in all of its possessions.

James G. Birney, an Alabama planter, freed his slaves in 1834. He led the American Anti-Slavery Society and in 1840 was the presidential candidate of the Liberty Party, which advocated the abolition of slavery.

Sarah and Angelina Grimke were from South Carolina and as young women they became active in the anti-slavery crusade. They were particularly effective in talking to women's groups which met under the guise of being "literary societies", "garden clubs", and "sewing circles".

Charles Stewart, an English abolitionist, had a profound effect on the abolitionist cause in the United States. John Brown's violent anti-slavery protests led him to the gallows after an unsuccessful attempt to capture the United States arsenal at Harper's Ferry, Virginia.

Frederick Augustus Washington Bailey was born a slave. A bright student, he was educated by his master's wife, Mrs. Thomas Auld. In 1838, when he was twenty-one, Frederick Bailey escaped to Massachusetts and changed his name to Frederick Douglass. In time he became a fiery orator against the evils of slavery. In his later years he served in the United States government in a number of distinguished positions.

In 1827 the small number of slaves in New York were freed. One of them vowed to work for the freedom of all slaves. She could not read or write, but she was a natural and moving speaker. She took the name Sojourner Truth. Wearing a banner which read, "Proclaim liberty throughout the land unto all the inhabitants thereof," Sojourner Truth spent her life going around the country preaching the evils of slavery to all who would listen.

The voices of the abolitionists would not be stilled. They intended to topple the hated institution of slavery. Instead, they were, in a few years, to destroy the union.

TO THINK ABOUT: Answer these questions on a separate sheet of paper.

1. What is the source of the motto used by Sojourner Truth?
2. Read this poem carefully:
    "They drag the Negro from his native shore,
    Make him a slave, and then his fate deplore;
    Sell him in distant countries and when sold,
    Revile the buyers but retain the gold."
    a. Who are "they" in the first line?
    b. From what section of the country do you think the poet came?
    c. What does revile mean?   d. What do you think the poet is trying to say in this poem?
3. a. What was Turner's Revolt? b. Why did this event make the South hate the abolitionists?

 MILLIKEN PUBLISHING CO.

Name _____ Date _____

A FINAL TEST AND REVIEW-I

Directions: In each of the following groups one item does not belong. Underline the item which does not belong and in the space provided explain why it does not belong.

1. a. Napoleon   b. Talleyrand   c. L'Ouverture

_____

2. a. Tecumseh   b. Creek   c. Cherokee

_____

3. a. James Madison   b. Henry Clay   c. Felix Grundy

_____

4. a. Henry Dearborn   b. William Eustis   c. William Hull

_____

5. a. William Henry Harrison   b. Winfield Scott   c. Oliver Perry

_____

6. a. Detroit   b. York   c. Baltimore

_____

7. a. *Constitution*   b. *Old Ironsides*   c. *United States*

_____

8. a. Sweden   b. Tripoli   c. China

_____

9. a. *Flying Cloud*   b. *Empress of China*   c. *Columbia*

_____

10. a. James Hargreaves   b. Elias Howe   c. Richard Arkwright

_____

11. a. Oliver Evans   b. John Fitch   c. Francis Lowell

_____

12. a. 1812   b. 1824   c. 1828

_____

13. a. cotton gin   b. sewing machine   c. mass production

_____

14. a. New Orleans   b. Mobile   c. Charleston

_____

15. a. John C. Calhoun   b. Patrick Henry   c. Thomas Jefferson

_____

16. a. Benjamin Lundy   b. Nat Turner   c. William Lloyd Garrison

_____

17. a. Frederick Douglass   b. Sojourner Truth   c. Angelina Grimke

_____

Name _____ Date _____

A FINAL TEST AND REVIEW—II

Directions: Fill in each blank to make a true statement.

1. James Monroe and _____ negotiated the purchase of Louisiana.

2. The Louisiana Purchase did not include the disputed land called _____.

3. The _____, passed in 1807, kept American ships from sailing to foreign ports.

4. The practice of _____ forced Americans to serve in the British navy.

5. The _____ was called to protest the War of 1812.

6. _____ attempted to unite the Indian tribes of the frontier.

7. Andrew Jackson and _____ were victorious at the Battle of New Orleans.

8. The Treaty of _____ ended the War of 1812.

9. In 1823 the _____ stated that the United States would not allow any new foreign colonies in the Western Hemisphere.

10. _____ opened trade between the United States and China.

11. _____ led the successful attack on Tripoli which ended the war with the Barbary pirates.

12. _____ is a whale product which is used in the manufacture of perfume.

13. The _____ changed all manufacturing from hand-made to machine-made.

14. _____'s invention made clothing cheaper to produce.

15. The _____ was favored by New England but opposed by the South.

16. The _____ marked the boundary between Maryland and Pennsylvania.

17. Monrovia, the capital of _____, was named in honor of James Monroe.

18. The _____ wanted all slavery to end at once.

19. The _____ consisted of the land that is now Alabama, Mississippi, and Louisiana.

20. Eli Whitney became wealthy as a result of his idea for _____.

21. _____ published *The Liberator*, a successful abolitionist newspaper.

22. "Proclaim liberty throughout the land—" was part of the motto used by _____

_____.

23. _____ led the fight against the abolitionists and the high tariff.

24. _____ composed "The Star Spangled Banner."

MILLIKEN PUBLISHING CO.

HISTORY WORDS TO KNOW

WORD	DEFINITION

28

MILLIKEN PUBLISHING CO.